I0164118

BAIT
AND
OTHER POEMS

BY S.E. MCKENZIE

Copyright © 2016 S. E. McKenzie
All rights reserved.
ISBN- 978-1-77281-028-8

ISBN-10: 1772810282

DEDICATION
To everyone who has been left out in the cold

THIS BOOK IS A BOOK OF SPECULATIVE FICTION
Characters, companies, governments, places, events, are either
products of the author's imagination or used fictitiously. Any
resemblance to persons (living or dead), companies, governments,
places and/or events, is a coincidence and unintentional.

TABLE OF CONTENTS

BAIT

BAIT

I

To defy the odds;
To do the impossible
Just to make it possible.

You hear the whistle call
To climb the wall;
That wall that blocked

The unknown to progress;
Uncertainty was the bait
For the nouveau prison state.

The wall
To block outsiders;
The wall

To empower insiders;
The wall
We had to climb

To save Reason
From being tried
For treason.

The ice caps melted away;
The seasons could not stay;
As the earth's axis tilted

Towards my land;
You held my hand
Without any demand

We grew strong
In a new world
Where risk and uncertainty

Felt so wrong;
Fear of the unknown
Weakened the strong.

The fear of the unknown
Made Toxic Man
Take control.

Without a smile
He screamed
Without a smile

His touch
Was harsh
And callous;

Toxic Man
Fed Malice
Which imprisoned

Hope
Under false pretense.
Without Hope

Love made no sense;
While Toxic Man
Glared and stared

For he had lost his magnetism
A long time ago
Now all he wanted was control.

The sky began to change
And many wondered why;
As the ice caps melted away

While Willful Blindness
Could not see
The new; so stuck

In a time gone by
When the Polar Regions
Had much more ice.

II

The Earth's axis began to sway.
Old measurements
Which were so precise

Were no longer that way.

Old measurements
Were no longer exact
For the tilting axis

Changed that fact.

New shipping routes
Changed the power structure too
Throwing out old world order

For the new;

What was living
To feed the living
Was wilting away;

For the order of the seasons
Could not stay the same way;
For the changing sky

Made it that way.

So that we could be free
From all this fear
Systematic demons

Exploited to regress
What had been
And what could have been

If only the vision had been seen
In the cool morning light
Ghetto-speak made them fight.

III
Predator
Fed on the fish
That fed on the worm

Predator
Owned the sky
Never letting his prey get by.

To defy those things which intimidate;
And to make those things that should be,
Be; so that we can see

The goodness all around; grow
Into tomorrow;
Beyond the wall

That kept the changing world
Out of sight;
Ghetto speak made them fight;

Ignorance stayed below
In the cave;
Ignorance was not that brave;

Could not fly into the sky above
The pulsating sound
Left on the ground

Attracts his prey
In a world
That has lost its way.

IV

Noise screeches;
Harmony teaches;
Vibrations make waves;

Rhythmic
Skin drum
Sets the pace

For the race
Deciding who will win
Who will lose

The Sum Zero game;
On the food chain;
Life and pain;

Creates hysteria;
Watch the Bully Master
Throw a micro portion

Of his money in the air;
Peasants run with hands waving
Fight each other; a break from slaving

And that is all;
Who will climb the wall?
Who will remain on the ground and crawl?

We lost our seasons
As the axis tilted
The flowers wilted

As the ice caps melted
New routes for shipping were devised
Were advised.

Before the ice could melt;
We were so cold;
We were well preserved

We were told.

Hysteria when focused on everything
That does not relate
Mesmerizes

For not just gold
Glitters
When lost in the cold.

V

Iron age
Of Rage
Felt the pull

Felt the push
Some had so much
They always looked full

They cup ran over
And slammed against the wall;
That wall.

The wall we were hiding behind;
Clinging to hop
Just cope.

VI

Even Chaos was lost in this noise;
I heard a voice so faint
In my ear tell me not to fear;

The mask has been lifted
The axis has been shifted
From the center of the Universe

The spin
Led to lost seasons
No reasons

The flood
Turned fresh water
Into mud

While drinking the hero's blood.

THE END

S.E. McKENZIE

GHOST

GHOST

I

There was a land
Hidden in
Machiavelli Valley

Where rulers ruled
With an iron fist;
Everyone was put on a list.

So polarized
The axis
Was tilting;

And love could not grow
In all the fear
That was near, life was wilting.

Cold air was pumped in; everywhere
It was so cold;
Made us shiver and feel old.

We were all trapped in this land
Hidden in
Machiavelli Valley.

Disconnected
Alienated
Doctrinated to be strangers;

We were left to fight for crumbs
And overcome dangers;
While the peasant king

Felt so righteous, just a silly little man
Taking whatever he can;
Pushed away those he demanded loyalty from;

Now;
Music that spoke of love was canned;
Mail sent everyday was spammed.

And how they fought
Each other
For the little they got.

They were all pitted
Against each other
While the walls hid the rot.

Judges sent many away
To live in cells
And to work for free all day;

The righteous few threw crumbs to them
Through a slot in the door;
While love was buried somewhere below the floor,

Love remained true.

While the wall hid decay they knew no other way.
The ruler; was just a silly little man;
Ruling with an iron fist the best that he can;

Everyone was put on a list.
Heads bowed down;
Covered with a frown.

II
Once living behind a veil;
She was adorned by ornaments
From head to toe, felt like hell.

The veil hid her face;
The veil hid her beauty;
She was raised to do her duty.

III

She is now a Sad Ghost;
Spirit in the night
Taking flight

Out of sight.
Living in her host
She felt his might;

And he felt no pity;
For love was pure;
Electrifying energy;

Came from the heart;
Pulsating
All night.

Because she was dead
Nothing could be said;
For she was just a Spirit without mass.

She still knew the secret
That grew
And could not pass away.

The secret was here to stay;
Despite what they had to say;
It didn't matter,

It was just that way.

IV

At first no one could see
What such a life
Would grow to be.

Lost people without names,
Buried below our moving feet;
They move so we don't feel defeat.

After the storm the form
Felt no fear,
For Love was near.

As new life grew
It glowed in you
And what was true

Could not be said
For Ghost was dead.
Ghost clung onto her host's heart;

So she could feel it pound;
She preferred this
Than sleeping all alone in the ground;

Always knowing that life was round.

For all Ghost had to hold on to
Was love so true;
Magic that was never gone;

Sang in tune
To his skin drum
Pounding strong and hard.

And Ghost would not let go

From the only world
That she would ever know.
She refused to stay forgotten

While sleeping
In the ground,
So she floated around;

Around the sun;
She yearned
She learned

Not to burn
As she walked
Between the flames

Scorching the earth;
For new life
Was about to begin.

V

At times
We did not have
Enough to eat

Though we knew
We would always meet
Again in a world without pain.

We could only see the heavens
In the night's sky;
For the morning sun

Brought too much light
Though the warmth gave us might
To stand upon our feet

Though we did not have enough to eat
We knew we would always meet
Again.

Upon this space below;
There was too much fear
For love to grow.

We felt the wind coming
From all directions
And we hid in the cave;

Not because we were not brave;
But it was time for us
To fall into a deep sleep.

VI

Ghost stayed awake
As she clung to her host's heart
She clung with all her might.

As he ran from the very place
Where she had died;
The place where so many had lied.

Ghost tried
To not be forgotten
And to live forever in memory.

No one knew the truth
Anymore.
We all knew

The story of her lost youth;
She clung to her host's heart
Just to feel the light

Illuminate
Free from hate
That sealed her fate.

To see the light;
We look up above
And see the face of space

In the night sky.
For Ghost could not leave
The land where she fell.

Without her host's help.
So he carried her away from hell.
They both lived above the ground

And below
The clouds.
Life grew, decayed and died.

The truth of this rhythm
Could not be denied.
Ghost felt objection

BAIT: Bonus Poems Included

But no one knew;
For they could not see her projection
And though her love was true

No one knew

Her lost attributes
Of creativity
For this was the age of destruction

And only a few
Knew
Ghost's gratitude.

As the axis was gaining tilt
Much was about to wilt.
While Ghost's love

Would be forever superior;
Ghost would no longer be treated
As the inferior.

Ghost had no reason
Accept to live in the moment
To enjoy each season

Ghost's joy could not be spoken;
When her host's power
Had awoken

For Ghost's love could not sleep
Yearned for immortality
And would not weep;

For Ghost clung
To her host's heart
And refused to let go;

While he carried her away
Inside of him
She would stay

And live as the day
Became tomorrow;
She hid from the shadows of sorrow;

For her love would live forever.
Bridging gaps
The way it was meant to be;

While the willfully blind
Refused to see;
The truth was meant to be

Not yet ready to set us free.

For the truth could not be said
For Ghost was dead
And her head

Was buried deep below
Where the living seldom go
Unless they mine

Gold
And other precious metals
Until they grow old.

Unlike Ghost.
Ghost was hidden behind the wall
So no one heard her cry;

No one believed
Such righteous souls
Would lie.

Even when they watched her die.
We all knew,
Only love would act true.

Then we were told that she looked too bold,

So there was no room for her in the sky;
And that is why
Ghost clung onto her host

As they ran from there
Hoping to find someone kind
Beyond Machiavelli Valley.

VII

Ghost could not be seen
For she was living inside her dream
And her host could not leave her behind

Though her buried bones
Were deep in the ground
Never to be found

Ghost's force was turning
Still burning
Still yearning

Still learning
To make the world
A better place.

Then I heard Ghost say;

"We need to make it better today.
For today never ends;
And tomorrow takes too long to come.

For all we have is now.
To make things right."
She said before she floated away

Into the midnight light.

THE END

S.E. McKENZIE

CHIEF

CHIEF

I

Chief of Machiavelli valley on call,
In charge of relief behind his wall.
His actions are based on his belief

That higher power over others
Is his to snare;
Never to share. never to care;

Blowing cold air everywhere.

Chief makes others feel cold and small
While he takes it all;
Oppressor loves to see others crawl

Higher power over others
Who would never be considered brothers;
In Machiavelli valley.

He is the chief; oblivious to all the grief
He causes when he says you are fired
Now go away, he loves the power to demean.

Caused when he yells and screams
While intruding on sleepers' dreams.
His cold air is everywhere.

Chief says he really does care
For the social welfare of all;
As he demands a higher wall.

Now there is no turning
Until you get to the top of the hill;
The place where they teach you

How to kill for a thrill;
On payday you can pay your bill
In Machiavelli valley.

II
The sun shines
Through the clouds
Only at variable times;

As Chief spreads his cold air everywhere.
He looks at you
As if you are not there;

His angry tone
Controls fate
Contributes to his estate.

Chief blames others
He would never call brothers;
For make believe crimes;

Such trouble gives him authority

To shoot on command;
Does not have to relate;
No empathy building to date;

For the road with no turn
Channels the flow
To the new city; so afraid it may burn.

We all hold on
To see the morning light;
Even though we are picked on;

By the elite who are paid to fight
And process
The regression creating a new recession,

Up on the hill;
The place where pretty faces
Greet you and shake your hand

Before they kill you
On command
In Machiavelli Valley.

Absolute power is Chief's only hope
To cope
As he ages; he rages

Blowing his cold air everywhere

Even at those sitting in the sun
Peeking out through the cloud
At variable times.

As chief gets his power
When he accuses others
Never called brothers, of make believe crimes;

As his power grows;
His wealth shows;
On display, for all to see;

From his tower
Of power
Sits a flower

Reminds him of the lady with the rose
Who arose; she knows;
As she grows

Still frozen in time
While chief
Blows cold air everywhere.

Chief would have it all while others had none.
Chief is a sad man
Lets his anger grow out of control,

To abuse, to use, to misuse;
A way of life; to oppress for fun;
While there is no turning you must run

Until you have found
The new city
Which breeds and feeds from war.

There you will be greeted
By a pretty face
Who would just love to splatter

Your blood all over the place.

Hate grows and needs relief
And the chief
Grows oblivious to the grief;

Deceit hid what was yet to come
On the road of no turning
Just burning without learning;

Repeating history;
Power just for the few,
Leaving the rest in misery.

Optimism for a fool;
Pessimism works for those that rule;
Spilling blood makes them drool;

Up on the hill
Where they learn to kill
For a thrill.

On payday
You get to pay your bill
In Machiavelli Valley

Where they have no promises to keep;
They might kill you in your sleep;
Leaving your loved ones all alone to weep.

III

Chief's power is fixed in a charade;
He is the happiest when he is on parade.
He yells and screams

Just to destroy her dreams;
For her happiness
Makes him envious;

His anger grows
Toxic and venomous;
He creates problems out of nothing at all

So that he has an excuse
To build a wall;
An excuse to ghettoize

S.E. McKENZIE

Others until they feel so small.

Culture of anger empowers his schemes;
He puts out the pressure
And destroys her dreams.

"More for me," he says in glee;
He counts his gold
And pile of cash

While he hides it all in his stash
In a drawer, on his side of the wall;
Leaving others with nothing at all.

He sits on his throne
Reading magazines
Pictures of girls he will never know

While he grows treasure;
For his pleasure;
Value that he can measure.

IV

Chief blames the aggregate;
He wants to segregate
The haves from the have nots.

He doesn't know how things work;
He yells and screams and acts like a jerk;
For his culture of anger seems to work.

He blames the woman with the rose
He grows problems
From nothing real at all

So he can build his wall.
He accuses; he abuses;
He never allows her in, or to begin.

V

Chief speaks of revolution
And the final solution;
While he keeps the air cold

And unpleasant;
His tyranny
Is forever present;

While super bombs
Are detonated
He wonders why he is so hated.

Even though he says that love is over rated.
He wishes that he could be part of the scene
He sees in his magazine.

He lives in a mansion
And has a few more;
He has objects of luxury

Piled from ceiling to floor
While locking out his creditor
Standing behind his armored door.

For his creditor is demanding more.
Chief knows what he owes
But can still get more

The way he has done
Many times before.
While others have hardly anything at all

He lives his life of luxury
Behind his wall.
Air he pumps out is too cold and too hot

You say anything you might get shot.

And near-slaves work
Just to eat
While he yells out

"Accept defeat."
Nothing will grow
In the place we will force you to go.

Culture of anger dominates;
As he stomps his boots, he agitates;
Nothing matches his expensive suits; he aggregates.

Within his culture of anger; he delegates
The lady with the rose; who arose as she grows.
Chief never lets her in;

So she has nowhere to begin.
Many say Chief is a jerk,
But they tremble when he is near,

His manufactures anger
So he can rule by fear.
He wasn't too smart

When he closed his heart;
Now he is willing to tear others apart.
He manufactures conflict

Out of nothing at all
So he can build
His multi-billion dollar wall.

Hear him scream;
See him destroy the dream
His face is distorted when he looks so mean.

During this time that many try to economize
He attacks them with stereotypical lies,
Waiting to hear their cries

As the dream wilts away and dies.
His generals eat well
While they plan a living hell;

As he builds his wall
Between the haves and have nots;
Things that can't grow; will decay then rot.

Chief does not know how things work;
He gets by because he acts like a jerk;
He never lets her in; nowhere for her to begin;

No entry point;
"And why should there be,"
He yells and shouts out;

"There will be more just for me."

Legislated poverty
Contributes to his wealth
While he brags about his health.

He fears those who have forbidden knowledge;
The tool for those who refuse
To be treated like a fool.

Forbidden knowledge;
The power of vision and sight;
Gained while reading all night

In artificial light.

S.E. McKENZIE

Chief's belief leads to grief;

While the lady holding on to the rose
Holds on with all her might
She waits for the morning light;

The lady with the rose arose and grows.

So strong, Chief won't let her in
She has nowhere to begin.
And all he can see is her skin.

THE END

SCORNED

SCORNED
I

Born into a world that was torn
By Slander and Division,
Fragile Ego; opposing position;

Could never make a good decision
Their scope of vision
Was so narrow it caused sorrow;

Many were caught up in the moment
And forgot
About Tomorrow.

Making each other's lives as hard as can be;
So willfully blind, they could not see;
The Malice was started

In the very cold hearted as they manipulate;
Emotionally charged into the Negative State;
How they loved the power of their growing Slander and Hate.

Without Equity; turned others into the Enemy;
Creating Negative Chemistry;
Emotionally charged; almost in Ecstasy;

Negative Bias
Fed a polarized world of Slander and Division;
Self-fulfilling prophecy; manufactured this condition.

In a roundabout way every day;
They fed Negative Bias so it never went away;
Fools believed everything Bias had to say;

For Negative Bias
Came before the Fall;
For it made fools out of nothing true at all.

Kept Life's disappointments at bay;
Fed Negative Bias
And defamed every day.

Hoping that those they hated
With all their Heart, would soon be part
Of the Departed.

To escape scorn, we were too willing to be torn;
Never needing to be warned;
Under the design of the Glass Ceiling.

We knew Negative Bias was always feeding;
And we would die too soon;
But for Negative Bias, it was never soon enough.

Our Enemy gave us a ladder to climb;
So that we could reach higher in Time;
If Time were only on our side.

Even though the Glass Ceiling cuts our flesh.
Our Free Spirit moves us along
Invisible to Negative Bias so near us and so wrong.

While many volunteered to be deleted
We refused to be defeated'
We exist with a right to be, you and me,

Which could transcend
Beyond expectations.
Visible in mass

Brick by brick
The wall grew to be
Less transparent; made Context harder to see;

Scope of Vision
So narrow
They could never be free;

So they allowed Negative Bias
To control
Their Destiny.

Worshipped by the Heir Apparent;
Rigid, frigid, no positive feeling;
Only way out was through the Glass Ceiling;

Negative Bias;
It stared, it glared, it shared;
Was always ready for feeding;

While you were smashing through the Glass Ceiling;
You were hurting but ignored all feeling;
Slander and Division; futile to resist

For only a few would ever be missed;
Most were trapped in the feeding
Of the Negative Bias so near us.

The Power Clique owned it all;
Loved to make others crawl
And feel small before the Fall.

You must play their game and that is all.
Don't let them know how you feel;
For they will kick you down again;

Why should they care?
After they destroy their targets,
They are out of there.

The Enemy gives purpose
And a ladder to climb;
Now you can say "I am who I am."

As you smash through the Glass Ceiling
Negative Bias
Always needs feeding.

For you to escape all the Unfair Dealing
You must climb and avoid distraction.
While they get so much satisfaction

BAIT: Bonus Poems Included

When they say with nose in the air
"We will make your life really hard,
For we own it all and we don't care,

We can make you crawl
For we owe you nothing at all."
They warned; they scorned;

While Goodwill's heart was broken in two;
There was not much
Anyone could do;

For it was all rigged in Negative Bias.

"As you get upset;
We will hang up the phone;
Leave you all alone;

For you know;
There is one way out,"
They said with scorn;

But they were wrong; we were strong;

Only way out was through the Glass Ceiling;
We would be cut and torn;
We were too aware that we didn't care;

Even though life is round for ever more
We arose from the ground
To be devastated no more;

And what was manipulated
Will pass in Machiavelli Valley,
While some of it remains

In ruins; still, there are gains;
Temporary life
Comes before Death

Existence without breath.
That day we dread;
Gone; we are dead.

To lie so still
Against one's will
After living life's power

In motion
Moving
So alive on a planet

BAIT: Bonus Poems Included

We never chose;
But lived on; never as one;
Always to be opposed by opposition

Slander and Division;
Toxic for the human condition
Lying in the Superior Position.

The miracle of it all.
The wonder is forgotten
When hunger pangs strike.

Man's cruelty to man
Invisible, ignores content;
Assumes intent;

Manufactured consent
To keep divided
What should have been whole.

The love of gold before the Fall
Brought us doom;
Such love pulled us into opposing directions.

At times we could not choose our selections.
The moment would pass
Forgotten, it could never last.

For we were so slight
Pitted against the might
Which was always out of sight;

The Mysterious Force
Behind it all could never be seen;
Some wondered if it had ever been

More than just a dream.

How could such turmoil been overseen;
Suffering that we never chose
We were knocked down to the ground

Then we arose.

We were born;
Into a world so torn;
So much was already worn.

Our pangs of hunger
Controlled who we could be
What we could see

The beauty around us.
The world we know
Had a mysterious source

In time
So long ago
How were we to know?

II
Energy that thrives
Keeps us alive
Gives us drive; to stay

And struggle for another day.

Even though they like to say so
They fill your mind with worry
Slander and division;

Unmanaged uncertainty
Makes it hard
To make a decision.

They are always in a hurry;
They own what you never will;
No stakeholder theory here;

Just fear; on the road with no turn;
Living in a city
Just waiting to burn.

III
Dark bands
Invisible Hands
Such a Force understands

We hope to see
The sea rush in
When high tide is due,

I will be waiting for you.

BAIT: Bonus Poems Included

We look through clouds
Until the atmosphere
Reaches space hoping to see a face

Of a life restored,
Somehow if it could be
Brought back to Earth.

But the Force we could not see
Would not let such a thing be;
Their return was forbidden.

For their time, like grains of sand

Had been spent
And controlled by the Invisible Hand.
So their life could never be lived again;

They would never return here
The place where they created so much fear
With their Slander and Division;

Beneath the atmosphere
Covering the ground
We could hear the harmony in all the sound.

Rules by their love of gold, their cold heart
Could still pound
And we wondered how.

The land was no longer ours;
Owned by the bank;
And hidden by walls;

We felt the connection anyway
For without the land
We would have nowhere to stand.

We hid behind the trees;
We saw our reflection
In the lake;

There was no mistake;
We were alive; we had survived;
So we were still able to be

Until we were alive no longer.

Starvation on this side of the wall
Was common
Though not seen at all.

BAIT: Bonus Poems Included

Paradise was everywhere and was not lost;
Just out of reach;
Never ours;

Owned by the bank
That kept paper bills
Which had written:

"In God We Trust"
All over them,
Near the ever-seeing eye.

The lie grew
Until many
Thought it must be true.

The walls hid what would be self-evident
If only could be seen;
Walls hid what once was;

For walls could never be transparent;
And walls were worshipped
By the Heir Apparent.

IV

We found a place still not ours
We stared at the moon for many hours
We slept amongst the flowers.

We knew we would die too soon;
For we lacked the paper which broke bias
For a moment, the ever-seeing eye would still deny us;

Disconnected from the Order
We could not die
Soon enough for them

While they bathed in Slander and Division
Allowed them to cloud
Their vision.

For the men of gold
Did not cherish love
For they were too cold.

While the land was left to grow back to nature
Until it was bought.
We knew if we were found there

We could be shot.
Wars between the haves and have nots
Continued to be true through history of misery.

The order, closed doors
To reason for others
Saved it for their chosen brothers.

Such decay in no man's land
Brought new life onto the Earth
But could never return the old.

From generation to generation
That is all we knew
And all we could see to be true

For the air around us
Was still transparent
And was there to share.

Death could not smile
It was just there
And we journeyed to it;

Every one of us
Would soon see the other side;
Maybe we would find mercy there;

For the world as we knew it was hostile to the poor;
And the bank changed locks on so many doors
We couldn't care anymore.

For we found our cave,
And returned to it
The way life might one day be

With purpose just to see.

V

Our feet march to war
Crushing flowers
Like many times before.

There was no harmony
And how could there be
For the Negative Bias controlled Destiny.

BAIT: Bonus Poems Included

Our heavy hearts pound
Until some are shot to the ground
Never to hear another sound.

We wait for a signal from the State
To end this madness
But it came too late.

Cities were designed to channel traffic one way;
Created wealth for some
In the usual way;

Slander and Division
Disconnected the Innocent
From the Final Decision with Suspicion.

They hated; they grated until the Nerves had awoken;
They could not scream out, they were too broken.
The Power Clique would use everything said

Against them; for Negative Bias was in control of their head;
We knew we would die too soon
For them it would never be soon enough.

Rigid was death in a world with too little love.
Paradise was paved
While the defamers said they would have saved

All those who confessed
To Slander and Division
Knew it was a terrible decision

To live under such Suspicion;

For Negative Bias
Had surrounded us
In this madness and Hell.

In their order it shaped every role;
And those without the paper
Of the ever-seeing-eye, would face Negative Bias

Alone; just another excuse to deny us;
While they gave us no privacy
In their conspiracy

Of Slander and Division.

BAIT: Bonus Poems Included

Many died too soon under Suspicion,
But not soon enough,
For those who did not care,

But wanted to own everywhere.
They demeaned with their angry tone
To scare those who were all alone;

For in this order;
Power would only flow
In one direction;

In Machiavelli Valley.

For the Enemy gave purpose
And a ladder
To climb.

While the mega walls stopped
Any kind of turning
On the narrow road;

Persecution
By Watchers
Was understood but not revealed.

S.E. McKENZIE

The divide between religion and science;
New and old;
Love of the Divine Right

And the pursuit of gold all night,

Led to much of the Earth being sold
To the highest bidder;
For the price of a dream and gold.

And we could hear their screams;
As they were reaching for their dreams;
Smashing through the Glass Ceiling;

Was the only way out.

THE END

Produced by S.E. McKenzie Productions
First Print Edition September 2016

Copyright © September 2016 by S. E. McKenzie
All rights reserved.

Enquiries: 1(778)992-2453
Mailing Address:
S. E. McKenzie Productions
168 B 5th St.
Courtenay, BC
V9N 1J4

Email Address:
messidartha@aol.com

http://www.amazon.com/SarahMcKenzie/e/B00H9RWX48/

www.ingramcontent.com/pod-product-compliance
Lightning Source LLC
Chambersburg PA
CBHW060535030426
42337CB00021B/4267